Voices of Change

VOICES
OF
CHANGE

Inspiring Words
from Activists Around the Globe

Edited by Kristen Hewitt

PRINCETON ARCHITECTURAL PRESS   NEW YORK

The crises that face communities around the globe are myriad, but so are the means to confront them. The words of wisdom in *Voices of Change* represent a great many ways to be an activist. They span from the nineteenth century to the present day, from abolitionists to suffragettes and early labor organizers, from the civil rights and gay liberation movements of the 1960s and 1970s to the Black Lives Matter movement of today. They range from Rachel Carson, who launched the modern-day environmental movement, to the youth climate movement led now by Greta Thunberg, Xiye Bastida, Isra Hirsi, and many others. Among the activists here are organizers, educators, lawyers, scientists, students, and writers. They are united by their creativity, their persistence, and their visions for a just and compassionate world.

I was inspired to create this collection by the guidance and encouragement I have always found in the words of other activists. I find in them a kind of sustenance, even when progress seems unfathomably slow.

Sometimes, change brought about by public outcry happens quickly, as in the Black Lives Matter protests following the murders of George Floyd, Breonna Taylor, and countless others, which caused a rapid shift in collective consciousness. The slow change happening in the moments between such outpourings of energy is not to be underestimated however.

Incremental shifts in culture and institutions parallel the internal changes happening in people's hearts and minds in response to new ideas and ways of thinking, acts of protest, and new understandings of what *justice* can mean. In this book, you'll find both calls to action for moments of energy and crisis as well as reminders to keep working in the lulls in between.

Some of the words in this book have given life to a whole new way of thinking—such as the idea of "intersectionality," coined by lawyer and civil rights advocate Kimberlé Williams Crenshaw, which refers to the way that forms of discrimination (i.e., race, class, and gender identity) are overlapping and interdependent and must be understood together in order to dismantle them.

Sometimes words form a mantra—a reminder to keep going when we are discouraged—that we can carry with us, like labor leader Dolores Huerta's words: "Every minute [is] a chance to change the world."

Sometimes words are an expression of excitement, anger, or energy, forming a rallying cry that can galvanize us into motion at a critical moment or tipping point. Sometimes they remind us that actions often do speak louder than words. Civil rights activist Bayard Rustin tells us that the "very act of protest confers dignity."

Perhaps one of the most exciting discoveries gleaned in the process of gathering these quotes is how they speak to each other across decades or even centuries.

Asmaa Mahfouz, an Egyptian activist, demonstrated in Cairo's Tahrir Square in 2011 during the Egyptian Revolution, galvanizing others to join her—"I am not scared, I will not be silenced, and I will continue to take to the streets." In her words I hear civil rights activist Rosa Parks, who refused to give up her seat during the Montgomery boycotts: "Knowing what must be done does away with fear."

Or consider Colin Kaepernick, who inspired a wave of protests in professional sports by refusing to kneel during the national anthem—"I am not going to stand up to show pride in a flag for a country that oppresses Black people and people of color," he said, echoing the first Black Major League Baseball player and civil rights activist Jackie Robinson, who wrote, decades earlier, "I cannot stand and sing the anthem. I cannot salute the flag."

Today's activists draw on a great lineage to fuel their work. Likewise, I hope you will find in this collection of quotes solidarity with voices of change, past and present, to sustain your own commitment to action, in whatever form that takes.

I am so grateful to all of the activists in this book for their leadership and work to bring about justice, in all of its forms. My thanks, too, go to my colleagues at Princeton Architectural Press for supporting this book, and for sharing with me the words and activists who have inspired each of them—this was truly a collaborative effort. Thanks especially to Abby Bussel, Ben English, Parker Menzimer, and Michelle Meier for their tireless work on this project. —Kristen Hewitt

ANOTHER WORLD
IS NOT ONLY POSSIBLE,
SHE IS ON HER WAY.

ON A QUIET DAY,
I CAN HEAR
HER BREATHING.

Arundhati Roy

Arundhati Roy (1961–) is an award-winning Indian author and
activist involved in environmental and human rights issues.
Her books include *The God of Small Things*, which won
the Man Booker Prize for Fiction in 1997.

The only way to support a revolution is to make your own.

Abbie Hoffman

Abbie Hoffman (1936–1989) was
a counterculture activist, cofounder
of the Youth International Party (Yippies),
and author of *Steal This Book* (1971).

Liberation is conceived by our imagination, carried in our hearts, and birthed through our revolutionary madness.

Talila A. Lewis

Talila A. Lewis (1986–) is an abolitionist community lawyer, educator, organizer who unites movements for justice by making manifest the inextricable links between ableism, racism, classism, and all forms of systemic and structural inequity and oppression.

I am not free while any woman is unfree, even when her shackles are very different from my own.

Audre Lorde

Audre Lorde (1934–1992) was an author, activist, and librarian who referred to herself as a "Black, lesbian, mother, warrior, poet." In her seminal writings, including *Zami* and *Sister Outsider*, Lorde argued for intersectionality in feminist discourse and critiqued "first-world feminism." Her work and enduring legacy informed third-wave feminism in the 1990s.

If anyone thinks he has no responsibilities,
it is because he has not sought them out.

Mary Lyon

Mary Lyon (1797–1849) was a pioneering educator
and advocate for women's education in the United States.
She founded the Mount Holyoke Female Seminary
(operating today as Mount Holyoke College).

Civil rights march, Selma, Alabama, 1965

ORGANIZE! AGITATE! EDUCATE! MUST BE OUR WAR CRY.

Susan B. Anthony

Susan B. Anthony (1820–1906) was a lifelong activist, reformer, and publisher, best known for leading the charge on women's suffrage in the United States, a struggle that culminated in the passage of the 19th Amendment in 1920. Anthony was an anti-slavery activist from a young age, and became active in the temperance movement.

Real poverty

*is the belief that the purpose
of life is acquiring wealth
and owning things.*

Real wealth

is not the possession of property but the recognition that our deepest need, as human beings, is to keep developing our natural and acquired powers to relate to other human beings.

Grace Lee Boggs

Grace Lee Boggs (1915–2015) was a Chinese American author, social activist, philosopher, intersectional feminist, and a noted figure in Detroit's civil rights and Black Power movements. She is author of *The Next American Revolution: Sustainable Activism for the Twenty-First Century*.

POWER IS NOT

BRUTE FORCE AND MONEY;

POWER IS IN YOUR SPIRIT.

POWER IS IN YOUR SOUL.

IT IS WHAT YOUR ANCESTORS,

YOUR OLD PEOPLE GAVE YOU.

POWER IS IN THE EARTH;

IT IS IN YOUR RELATIONSHIP

TO THE EARTH.

Winona LaDuke

Winona LaDuke (1959–) is an activist, environmentalist, and economist. Her work centers on the rights of Indigenous peoples including the Ojibwe of present-day Minnesota, from whom LaDuke is partly descended. She founded the Indigenous Women's Network and the White Earth Land Recovery Project, and is executive director of Honor the Earth.

We are on Earth to take care of life.

We are on Earth to take care of each other.

Xiye Bastida

Xiye Bastida (2002–) is an environmentalist and member of the Mexican Indigenous Otomi-Toltec nation. Bastida began advocating for progessive climate policy after immigrating to the United States in 2015. She organizes strikes and actions with Fridays for Future and is a member of the youth-led climate group Sunrise Movement.

Vietnam War protest, Washington, DC, 1967

But we do not merely protest; we make renewed demand for freedom in that vast kingdom of the human spirit where freedom has ever had the right to dwell: the expressing of thought to unstuffed ears; the dreaming of dreams by untwisted souls.

W. E. B. Du Bois

W. E. B. Du Bois (1968–1963) was a writer, academic, educator, and anti-racist activist whose work greatly influenced civil rights and the fight for Black equality in the nineteenth and twentieth centuries. Du Bois was the first Black graduate of Harvard University and cofounder of the NAACP. He is the author of *The Souls of Black Folk* among other seminal texts.

When an individual is protesting society's refusal to acknowledge his dignity as a human being, his very act of protest confers dignity on him.

Bayard Rustin

Bayard Rustin (1912–1987) was an activist, labor organizer, and proponent of nonviolence whose work centered race and class struggles. A pivotal poltical figure who influenced Dr. King, Rustin nevertheless carried out much of his work behind the scenes. Rustin advocated for gay rights in the 1980s.

Saying "Black Lives Matter" both literally and figuratively restores people's dignity.

Alicia Garza

Alicia Garza (1981–) is an Oakland-based organizer, civil rights activist, writer, and public speaker known for cofounding the Black Lives Matter movement. She currently directs special projects at the National Domestic Workers Alliance and is the principal at the Black Futures Lab.

Hong Kong protests, 2019

DON'T FEEL GUILTY.

Do something to make it better. Help us heal by standing— or sitting—alongside us.

Michael Bennett

Michael Bennett (1985–) is a former professional football player and free agent for the NFL as well as an activist who has used his platform in support of Black rights and the Black Lives Matter movement. He has played for the Seattle Seahawks and the New England Patriots, among others. He is author of the memoir *Things That Make White People Uncomfortable*.

Trans people are extraordinary, strong, intelligent, persistent, and resilient. We have to be. And we will not stand for the picking and choosing of rights. We still have hope.

Sage Grace Dolan-Sandrino

Sage Grace Dolan-Sandrino (2000–) is an Afro-Latinx artist, public speaker, and organizer who became an activist when she came out to the world as trans at the age of thirteen. Under the Obama administration, she helped to create federal guidance for protecting trans students from discrimination. She has written for the *Washington Post* and *Teen Vogue*.

Define yourself in your own terms. In terms of gender, race, anything. We are not what other people say we are. We are who we know ourselves to be, and we are what we love.

Laverne Cox

Laverne Cox (1972–) is an Emmy-nominated actress, documentary film producer, and equal rights advocate. She is the first trans woman of color to have a leading role on a mainstream scripted television show, in her role as Sophia Burset in *Orange Is the New Black*.

No great idea in its beginning can ever be within the law. How can it be within the law? The law is stationary. The law is fixed. The law is a chariot wheel which binds us all regardless of conditions or place or time.

Emma Goldman

Emma Goldman (1869–1940) was an anarchist political activist and writer. Born in Russia to a Jewish family, she emigrated to the United States in 1885. Goldman was an early advocate of free speech, women's equality, and labor. She was imprisoned and deported for speaking out against conscription during World War I. She is author of *Anarchism and Other Essays*.

Protest that endures, I think, is moved by a hope far more modest than that of public success: namely, the hope of preserving qualities in one's own heart and spirit that would be destroyed by acquiescence.

Wendell Berry

Wendell Berry (1934–) is a novelist, poet, essayist, environmental activist, cultural critic, and farmer who lives in Kentucky. He is author of over forty books, including *The Mad Farmer Poems*, *Sex, Economy, Freedom and Community*, and *Our Only World*.

César Chávez, 1979

When we are really honest with ourselves we must admit our lives are all that really belong to us.

So it is how we use our lives that determines the kind of men we are.

César Chávez

César Chávez (1927–1993) was a union leader, labor organizer, and Latinx American civil rights activist who dedicated his life to improving treatment, pay, and working conditions for farm workers. With Dolores Huerta, he founded the National Farm Workers Association (NFWA).

I call on people to be "obsessed citizens," forever questioning and asking for accountability. That's the only chance we have today of a healthy and happy life.

Ai Weiwei

Ai Weiwei (1957–) is an artist and human rights activist from Beijing, China, known for political artworks, installations, and videos. In April 2011, Weiwei was arrested by Chinese authorities and held for three months. Since 2015, to escape persecution, he has been a refugee and now lives in England. His recent works include *Human Flow*, a documentary exploring the global refugee crisis.

Go to where the silence is

and say something.

Amy Goodman

Amy Goodman (1957–) is a journalist and investigative reporter and the cohost and executive producer of *Democracy Now! The War and Peace Report*, a progressive daily news program, which she cofounded in 1996. She is author of many books, including *The Exception to the Rulers: Exposing Oily Politicians, War Profiteers, and the Media That Love Them* and *Breaking the Sound Barrier*.

I cannot stand and sing the anthem.

I cannot salute the flag; I know that I am a Black man in a white world.

Jackie Robinson

Jackie Robinson (1919–1972) joined the Brooklyn Dodgers as first baseman in 1947, becoming the first Black man to play in Major League Baseball (MLB) since 1889, when baseball became segregated. He was active in the civil rights movement and he helped establish the Freedom National Bank, a Black-owned financial institution that was based in Harlem, New York.

I am not going to stand up to show pride in a flag for a country that oppresses Black people and people of color.

Colin Kaepernick

Colin Kaepernick (1987–) is a football quarterback and anti-racist activist whose refusal to stand during the US national anthem divided the sports community and inspired a wave of protests in professional sports in the latter half of the 2010s. Kaepernick has criticized systemic racism, racial inequality, and police brutality. A free agent, Kaepernick previously played for the San Francisco 49ers.

Anti-draft demonstration, Washington, DC, 1970

YOU MEASURE DEMOCRACY BY THE FREEDOM IT GIVES ITS DISSIDENTS,

NOT THE FREEDOM IT GIVES ITS ASSIMILATED CONFORMISTS.

Abbie Hoffman

Abbie Hoffman (1936–1989) was
a counterculture activist, cofounder
of the Youth International Party (Yippies),
and author of *Steal This Book* (1971).

Wherever men or women are persecuted because of their race, religion, or political views, that place must— at that moment— become the center of the universe.

Elie Wiesel

Elie Wiesel (1928–2016) was a Romanian-born Jewish writer, professor, political activist, and Nobel laureate. The author of numerous books, he is well known for his memoir *Night*, based on his experiences as a prisoner in Nazi concentration camps during World War II.

There are two things I've got
a right to, and these are
Death or Liberty—one or the other
I mean to have.

No one will take me back alive;
I shall fight for my liberty.

Harriet Tubman

Harriet Tubman (c. 1822–1913) was an abolitionist born in the American South
who escaped slavery in 1849. Tubman directly and indirectly assisted over
100 enslaved people in their journeys along the Underground Railroad, an informal but
well-organized northward route secretly maintained by activists and abolitionists.

Every single one of us... can leave the next generation with a better reflection of their innate worth and their inherent power simply by claiming and living in our own power.

America Ferrera

America Ferrera (1984–) is an actress, outspoken immigration activist, and founding member of the TIME'S UP Legal Defense Fund, created in 2018 by women in the entertainment industry in response to Harvey Weinstein's criminal sexual acts and the #MeToo movement.

Our struggle then must begin with the reappropriation of our body, the revaluation and rediscovery of its capacity for resistance, and expansion and celebration of its powers, individual and collective.

Silvia Federici

Silvia Federici (1942–) is an Italian American feminist activist, writer, and teacher. She cofounded the International Feminist Collective and has been active in the anti-globalization and the US anti-death-penalty movements. She is professor emerita and teaching fellow at Hofstra University. Her best-known book is *Caliban and the Witch: Women, the Body and Primitive Accumulation*.

Iraqi anti-government demonstrators,
Tahrir Square, Baghdad, Iraq, 2019

EVERYONE SHOULD BE ABLE TO SEE THEMSELVES IN A MOVEMENT LIKE THIS, AND IF YOU DON'T, THEN THAT'S REASON TO MAKE THIS SPACE MORE INCLUSIVE.

Isra Hirsi

Isra Hirsi (2003–) is an environmental activist and cofounder of the US Youth Climate Strike, one of the largest climate mobilizations in US history. She is the daughter of US Congresswoman Ilhan Omar of Minneapolis, Minnesota, the first Somali American to hold her office.

The better we understand how identities and power work together from one context to another, the less likely our movements for change are to fracture.

Kimberlé Williams Crenshaw

Kimberlé Williams Crenshaw (1959–) is a lawyer, civil rights advocate, philosopher, and leading scholar of critical race theory who developed the theory of intersectionality. She is a professor at the UCLA School of Law and Columbia Law School, where she specializes in race and gender issues, and she cofounded the African American Policy Forum think tank.

National Organization for Women (NOW) and National Rainbow Coalition
in front of the White House, Washington, DC, 1996

A democracy cannot thrive where power remains unchecked and justice is reserved for a select few.

Ignoring these cries and failing to respond to this movement is simply not an option— for peace cannot exist where justice is not served.

John Lewis

John Lewis (1940–2020) was a civil rights leader who served as the US representative for Georgia's 5th Congressional District for more than three decades. The son of sharecroppers in the Jim Crow south, he survived a brutal beating by police during the 1965 march for voting rights in Selma, Alabama. He is known for his lifelong commitment to racial and social justice.

Not only must we know the arguments on all sides of any debate, we must also seriously consider the questions that are not being asked and their implications for everyone involved.

William J. Barber II

Reverend William J. Barber (1963–) is a protestant minister and political activist. A member of the national board of the NAACP and president of the North Carolina branch, he created the Forward Together Moral Monday Movement, leading the "Moral Monday" protests at the North Carolina legislature building beginning in 2013.

We have a serious problem with incarceration in this country. It's destroying families, it's destroying communities, and we're the most incarcerated country in the world. … When you look deeper and look at the reasons we got to this place, we as a society made some choices politically and legislatively, culturally, to deal with poverty, deal with mental illness in a certain way, and that way usually involves using incarceration.

John Legend

John Legend (1978–) is a singer, songwriter, pianist, and philanthropist who is the first Black man to win an EGOT: the Emmy, Grammy, Oscar, and Tony. Legend established the Show Me Campaign, which works to end cycles of poverty, the school-to-prison pipeline, and other pervasive, systemic issues through access to education.

FROM THE RIGHT TO KNOW AND THE DUTY TO INQUIRE FLOWS THE OBLIGATION TO ACT.

Sandra Steingraber

Sandra Steingraber, PhD (1959–), is a biologist, author, and environmental activist. She writes about climate change, ecology, and the links between human health and the environment. She is author of several books, including *Living Downstream*, in which she writes about surviving cancer in her twenties and the growing body of evidence linking cancer to environmental contamination.

The sad truth of the matter is that most evil is done by people who never made up their minds to be or do either good or evil.

Hannah Arendt

Hannah Arendt (1906–1975) was German-born American political scientist and philosopher best known for her study of totalitarianism. She is the author of many books, including *The Origins of Totalitarianism*, *The Human Condition*, and *Eichmann in Jerusalem: A Report on the Banality of Evil*.

Mother Jones, 1914

PRAY FOR THE DEAD AND FIGHT LIKE HELL FOR THE LIVING.

Mother Jones

Mary Harris Jones (1837–1930) was a union organizer, active proponent of limiting child labor, campaigner for the United Mine Workers Union, and founder of the Social Democratic Party in Ireland. She helped establish the Industrial Workers of the World in 1905.

We must stand together to resist, for we will get what we can take— just that and no more.

Rose Schneiderman

Rose Schneiderman (1882–1972) was a Polish-born Jewish American feminist, socialist, and union leader who played a significant role in labor organizing and the improvement of working conditions for women, and was a founding member of the American Civil Liberties Union.

POWER
CONCEDES
NOTHING
WITHOUT A DEMAND.
IT NEVER DID
AND IT NEVER WILL.

Frederick Douglass

Frederick Douglass (c. 1818–1895), author of *Narrative of the Life of Frederick Douglass, An American Slave* and other writings, was born into slavery in or around 1818. He became a prominent activist, social reformer, and leader in the abolitionist movement, which sought to end slavery, before and during the Civil War.

Martin Luther King Jr., 1964

Those of us who love peace must organize as effectively as the war hawks.

Martin Luther King Jr.

Martin Luther King Jr. (1929–1968) was a minister and civil rights activist who played a leading role in ending the legal segregation of Black citizens in the US and in enacting the Civil Rights Act of 1964 and the Voting Rights Act of 1965. A recipient of the Nobel Peace Prize, he was assassinated in 1968 in Memphis, Tennessee.

Every moment is an organizing opportunity, every person a potential activist, every minute a chance to change the world.

Dolores Huerta

Dolores Huerta (1930–) is a labor leader from New Mexico whose activism on behalf of the migrant farmworkers led to the establishment of the United Farm Workers (UFW), which she cofounded. A 2012 recipient of the Presidential Medal of Freedom, she continues to organize through the Dolores Huerta Foundation on behalf of the working poor, women, and children.

IF WE STAY
POSITIVE, INCLUSIVE, DEMOCRATIC,
WE HAVE A TRULY HISTORIC OPPORTUNITY TO BUILD A GLOBAL MOVEMENT FOR SOCIAL JUSTICE.

Medea Benjamin

Medea Benjamin (1952–) is a political activist and cofounder of CODEPINK, a women-led organization to prevent wars and militarism, as well as Global Exchange, an international human rights organization. She is the author of many books, most recently *The Kingdom of the Unjust: Behind the U.S.-Saudi Connection* and *Drone Warfare: Killing by Remote Control*.

EFFECTIVE LEADERS MUST BE TRUTH SEEKERS, AND THAT REQUIRES A WILLINGNESS TO UNDERSTAND TRUTHS OTHER THAN OUR OWN.

Stacey Abrams

Stacey Abrams (1973–) is a politician, lawyer, voting rights activist, and author who served in the Georgia House of Representatives and as minority leader. In 2018, she became the first Black woman in US history to win the gubernatorial nomination of either major party.

There is no partial commitment to justice.

You are either in or you're out.

John Carlos

John Carlos (1945–) is a former track and field athlete, professional football player, activist, and founding member of the Olympic Project for Human Rights (OPHR). He is known for his raised-fist salute, a symbol of Black Power alongside fellow athlete Tommie Smith, at the 1968 Olympics in Mexico City.

I have learned over the years that when one's mind is made up, this diminishes fear; knowing what must be done does away with fear.

Rosa Parks

Rosa Parks (1913–2005) was arrested in 1955 after she refused a bus driver's instructions to give up her seat to a white passenger on a bus in Montgomery, Alabama. This act sparked the Montgomery Bus Boycott, one of the earliest and most successful mass movements on behalf of civil rights in the US. It lasted 381 days and led to the end of racial segregation in the Montgomery public transit system.

I LEARNED THAT COURAGE WAS NOT THE ABSENCE OF FEAR, BUT THE TRIUMPH OVER IT.

THE BRAVE MAN IS NOT HE WHO DOES NOT FEEL AFRAID, BUT HE WHO CONQUERS THAT FEAR.

Nelson Mandela

Nelson Mandela (1918–2013) was a South African anti-apartheid leader who led a campaign of peaceful, nonviolent protest against the government and its policies. Mandela became the first Black president of South Africa from 1994 to 1999, after serving twenty-seven years in prison for political offenses.

Dakota Access Pipeline protest,
San Francisco, California, 2016

STANDING
ROCK
STAND UP TO BIG OIL
WATER
LIFE
MNI WICHONI
BACK-IN ANGLE PARKING ONLY
ATY RIGHTS

Burst down those closet doors once and for all, and stand up, and start to fight.

Harvey Milk

Harvey Milk (1930–1978), an activist and politician, became one of the first openly gay officials in the US, serving on San Francisco's Board of Supervisors in 1977. As a result of his work, the city council passed a Gay Rights Ordinance in 1978 that protected gays and lesbians from being fired from their jobs. Milk was assassinated later that same year.

IF YOU'RE NOT PISSING SOMEONE OFF, YOU'RE PROBABLY NOT DOING YOUR JOB.

Cecile Richards

Cecile Richards (1957–) is an abortion rights and women's rights activist who served as president of the Planned Parenthood Federation of America and Planned Parenthood Action Fund. An advocate for affordable access to reproductive healthcare, Richards is the author of *Make Trouble: Stand Up, Speak Out, and Find the Courage to Lead*.

ONE OF OUR GOALS IS TO REINVENT THE F-WORD: *FEMINISM.*

OUR MESSAGE: FIND YOUR OWN CRAZY, CREATIVE WAY TO BE A FEMINIST AND AN ACTIVIST.

Guerrilla Girls

The Guerrilla Girls (formed 1985) are activist artists who expose sexism, racism, and corruption in politics, art, film, and pop culture. Wearing gorilla masks and employing facts and figures in their street projects, posters, and stickers, the group uses subversive humor to make the public aware of current inequities.

A punk is someone who knows how to ask the world uncomfortable questions and does everything possible to make sure the world can't cop out of answering those questions. A punk is a person who lives and breathes astonishment.

Pussy Riot

Pussy Riot (formed 2011) is a Russian feminist punk rock and performance art collective that staged guerrilla performances in public places. In 2012 members were arrested, imprisoned, and denied bail, and their trial was repeatedly postponed, garnering international attention. They were granted amnesty and freed from prison after almost two years.

George Floyd protest against police brutality,
Dallas, Texas, 2020

Those who profess to favor freedom, and yet depreciate agitation, are men who want crops without plowing up the ground.

Frederick Douglass

Frederick Douglass (c. 1818–1895), author of *Narrative of the Life of Frederick Douglass, An American Slave* and other writings, was born into slavery in or around 1818. He became a prominent activist, social reformer, and leader in the abolitionist movement, which sought to end slavery, before and during the Civil War.

Do not put such unlimited power into the hands of the Husbands. Remember all Men would be tyrants if they could. If particular care and attention is not paid to the Ladies we are determined to foment a Rebellion, and will not hold ourselves bound by any Laws in which we have no voice, or Representation.

Abigail Adams

Abigail Adams (1744–1818), born in Massachusetts, was the wife of President John Adams and the mother of President John Quincy Adams. She is known for being a close, unofficial advisor to her husband, and for her early advocacy for women's rights, women's education, and the abolition of slavery.

Such a fine sunny day, and I have to go, but what does my death matter, if through us thousands of people are awakened and stirred to action?

Sophie Scholl

Sophie Scholl (1921–1943) was a German student and political activist who organized against the ascendant Nazi party with her White Rose resistance group. She was executed for treason by the Nazi party in 1943.

I think it only makes sense to seek out and identify structures of authority, hierarchy, and domination in every aspect of life, and to challenge them; unless a justification for them can be given, they are illegitimate, and should be dismantled, to increase the scope of human freedom.

Noam Chomsky

Noam Chomsky (1928–) is a professor, cognitive scientist, philosopher, social critic, and political activist best known for his contributions to the field of linguistics. He is the author of numerous books, including *Global Discontents: Conversations on the Rising Threats to Democracy* and *Optimism Over Despair: On Capitalism, Empire, and Social Change*.

THE HUMAN HEART IS THE FIRST HOME OF DEMOCRACY.

Terry Tempest Williams

Terry Tempest Williams (1955–) is a writer, activist, and environmentalist. The recipient of numerous awards including a John Simon Guggenheim Fellowship in creative nonfiction, she is the author of many books, most recently *The Hour of Land: A Personal Topography of America's National Parks* and *Erosion: Essays of Undoing*.

I AM NOT SCARED, I WILL NOT BE SILENCED, AND I WILL CONTINUE TO TAKE TO THE STREETS AND CRITICIZE ANY WRONGDOING THAT I SEE.

Asmaa Mahfouz

Asmaa Mahfouz (1985–) is an Egyptian activist and one of the founders of the April 6 Youth Movement, which sought to organize workers to protest low wages and high food prices. She is known for speaking out against the regime of Hosni Mubarak in an online video and calling others to join her in Tahrir Square, the focal point of the 2011 Egyptian Revolution.

The assumption that animals are without rights and the illusion that our treatment of them has no moral significance is a positively outrageous example of Western crudity and barbarity. Universal compassion is the only guarantee of morality.

Albert Schweitzer

Albert Schweitzer (1875–1965) was an Alsatian theologian, musician, writer, philosopher, humanitarian, and physician. The recipient of a Nobel Peace Prize in 1952, Schweitzer is best known for founding a hospital, together with his wife, Helen Bresslau, who was a nurse, at Lambaréné, modern-day Gabon in Central Africa.

DO NOT SNUFF
OUT THE DREAMS
OF
HISPANICS!
LCLAA

POBRES PARA
DARLE A
LOS RICOS

LCLAA

Migrant farm worker at demonstration,
Washington, DC, 1981

IF WE DON'T HAVE WORKERS ORGANIZED INTO LABOR UNIONS, WE'RE IN GREAT PERIL OF LOSING OUR DEMOCRACY.

Dolores Huerta

Dolores Huerta (1930–) is a labor leader from New Mexico whose activism on behalf of the migrant farmworkers led to the establishment of the United Farm Workers (UFW), which she cofounded. A 2012 recipient of the Presidential Medal of Freedom, she continues to organize through the Dolores Huerta Foundation on behalf of the working poor, women, and children.

There never will be complete equality until women themselves help to make laws and elect lawmakers.

Susan B. Anthony

Susan B. Anthony (1820–1906) was a lifelong activist, reformer, and publisher, best known for leading the charge on women's suffrage in the United States, a struggle that culminated in the passage of the 19th Amendment in 1920. Anthony was an anti-slavery activist from a young age, and became active in the temperance movement.

Never be deceived that
the rich will allow you
to vote away their wealth.

Lucy Parsons

Lucy Eldine González Parsons (c. 1853–1942) was born into slavery near Waco, Texas.
Both she and her husband, Albert Richard Parsons, were anarchists and labor organizers who
participated in the Haymarket Uprising of 1886 in Chicago. She was the founder of the newspaper
Freedom, which addressed issues such as labor organizing, lynching, and Black peonage.

When we identify where our privilege intersects with somebody else's oppression, we'll find our opportunities to make real change.

Ijeoma Oluo

Ijeoma Oluo (1980–) is a Nigerian American writer whose work addresses race and identity, feminism, social and mental health, social justice, and the arts. She is the author of *Mediocre: The Dangerous Legacy of White Male America* and *So You Want to Talk About Race*. Oluo has written for the *Guardian*, the *Stranger*, and the *Establishment*, where she is also an editor at large.

I BELIEVE THAT IN A MODERN, MORAL, AND WEALTHY SOCIETY, NO PERSON IN AMERICA SHOULD BE TOO POOR TO LIVE.

Alexandria Ocasio-Cortez

Alexandria Ocasio-Cortez (1989–), also known by her initials as AOC, is an American politician, electoral organizer, and activist serving as the US Representative for New York's 14th congressional district in the Bronx and Queens since 2019. She advocates for the working class over corporate interests, and works for social, racial, economic, and environmental justice.

Maxine Waters, 1998

I've seen a lot of poverty— coming up as a young child, lost hopes and dreams and people that never had a chance to have a decent quality of life.

I believe we can do a lot greater than that.

Maxine Waters

Maxine Waters (1938–), born in St. Louis, Missouri, serves as the US Representative for California's 43rd congressional district. Of her many accomplishments, she made history as the first woman and first Black chair of the House Financial Services Committee and works as an outspoken advocate for women, children, people of color, and the poor.

Helen Keller, 1914

The country is governed for the richest, for the corporations, the bankers, the land speculators, and for the exploiters of labour. Surely we must free men and women together before we can free women. The majority of mankind are working people. So long as their fair demands— the ownership and control of their lives and livelihood—are set at naught, we can have neither men's rights nor women's rights.

Helen Keller

Helen Keller (1880–1968) was an educator, activist, and advocate for the blind and deaf. She became the first deaf-blind person to earn a bachelor's degree, and later joined the Socialist Party of America and the Industrial Workers of the World. She cofounded the American Civil Liberties Union (ACLU).

There is no such thing as a single-issue struggle because we do not live single-issue lives.

Audre Lorde

Audre Lorde (1934–1992) was an author, activist, and librarian who referred to herself as a "Black, lesbian, mother, warrior, poet." In her seminal writings, including *Zami* and *Sister Outsider*, Lorde argued for intersectionality in feminist discourse and critiqued "first-world feminism." Her work and enduring legacy informed third-wave feminism in the 1990s.

Feminism has never been about getting a job for one woman.

It's about making life more fair for women everywhere.

It's not about a piece of the existing pie; there are too many of us for that.

It's about baking a new pie.

Gloria Steinem

Gloria Steinem (1934–) is a journalist, lecturer, political activist, and feminist organizer who was a leader and spokeswoman of the women's rights movements of the 1960s, 1970s, and 1980s. She was a columnist for *New York* magazine and cofounded *Ms.* magazine.

To girls everywhere,

I am with you. On nights when you feel alone, I am with you. When people doubt you or dismiss you, I am with you. I fought every day for you. So never stop fighting, I believe you.

Chanel Miller

Chanel Miller (1992–) is a writer and artist who spoke out about her sexual assault by Brock Turner at Stanford University in 2015. Her victim impact statement was read 11 million times in four days, inspiring changes in California law and the recall of the judge in the case. Her award-winning memoir is entitled *Know My Name*.

WE ARE ALWAYS STRONGER TOGETHER, SO IF WE CAN CONQUER DIVISION, WE CAN CONQUER ANYTHING.

Kenidra Woods

Kenidra Woods (2001–) is a gun-control and mental health advocate. She organized Hope for Humanity in St. Louis, Missouri, an event to connect students of different races and backgrounds and empower them to be better included and represented in the fight to end the epidemic of gun violence. Her memoir is entitled *A Heart of Hope*.

You can't be a feminist in the United States and stand up for the rights of the American woman and then say that you don't want to stand up for the rights of Palestinian women in Palestine. It's all connected.

Linda Sarsour

Linda Sarsour (1980–) is a Palestinian American activist who advocated for the civil rights of Arab Americans following the September 11th attacks and was a key organizer of the 2017 Women's March on Washington, DC. She served as executive director of the Arab American Association of New York.

Climate change is a man-made problem and must have a feminist solution.

Mary Robinson

Mary Robinson (1944–) is a lawyer, politician, and diplomat who served as president of Ireland from 1990 to 1997 and as UN High Commissioner for Human Rights from 1997 to 2002. In 2009, she was awarded the Presidential Medal of Freedom by Barack Obama. She now leads a foundation devoted to climate justice.

IF YOU ARE TRYING TO TRANSFORM A BRUTALIZED SOCIETY INTO ONE WHERE PEOPLE CAN LIVE IN DIGNITY AND HOPE, YOU BEGIN WITH THE EMPOWERING OF THE MOST POWERLESS.

YOU BUILD FROM THE GROUND UP.

Adrienne Rich

Adrienne Rich (1929–2012) was a poet, scholar, teacher, critic, and feminist whose work created discourse around the oppression of women and lesbians. Her works include *The Dream of a Common Language*, *An Atlas of the Difficult World*, *On Lies, Secrets, and Silence*, and "Compulsory Heterosexuality and Lesbian Existence."

Any analysis that does not take intersectionality into account cannot sufficiently address the particular manner in which Black women are subordinated.

Kimberlé Williams Crenshaw

Kimberlé Williams Crenshaw (1959–) is a lawyer, civil rights advocate, philosopher, and leading scholar of critical race theory who developed the theory of intersectionality. She is a professor at the UCLA School of Law and Columbia Law School, where she specializes in race and gender issues, and she cofounded the African American Policy Forum think tank.

For the sake of our psychic stability as well as our physical well-being we must be free men and exercise free choices. We must make decisions about our own destinies. We must be able to learn and profit from our own mistakes. Only then can we become competent and prosperous communities. We must be free in the most literal sense of the word— not sold or coerced into accepting programs for our own good, not of our own making or choice.

Clyde Warrior

Clyde Warrior (1939–1968) was an activist, orator, and cofounder of the National Indian Youth Council in the 1960s. Born in Ponca City, Oklahoma, and raised in Ponca traditions, Warrior spoke out against discrimination, poverty, and oppression in Native American communities.

If an Indian doesn't have land, he has nothing.

Lucy Friedlander Covington

Lucy Friedlander Covington (1910–1982) was a Native American tribal leader and political activist. A member of the Colville tribe, whose reservation is located in eastern Washington State, she worked to preserve tribal sovereignty and to bring an end to federal policies designed to take control of land and natural resources from tribal ownership.

To me, cruelty is the worst of human sins. Once we accept that a living creature has feelings and suffers pain, then if we knowingly and deliberately inflict suffering on that creature we are equally guilty. Whether it be human or animal we brutalize *ourselves*.

Jane Goodall

Jane Goodall (1934–) is a British primatologist and anthropologist, known for her long-term research on the chimpanzees of Gombe Stream National Park in Tanzania. She has worked extensively on conservation and animal welfare issues. She founded the Jane Goodall Institute and serves on the board of the Nonhuman Rights Project.

By acquiescing in an act that can cause such suffering to a living creature, who among us is not diminished as a human being?

Rachel Carson

Rachel Carson (1907–1964) was a writer, ecologist, and conservationist whose book *Silent Spring* warned of the dangers of chemical pesticides, catalyzing the global environmental movement and leading to the creation of United States Environmental Protection Agency.

The line that connects the bombing of civilian populations to the mountain removed by strip mining... to the tortured prisoner seems to run pretty straight. We're living, it seems, in the culmination of a long warfare— warfare against human beings, other creatures and the Earth itself.

Wendell Berry

Wendell Berry (1934–) is a novelist, poet, essayist, environmental activist, cultural critic, and farmer who lives in Kentucky. He is author of over forty books, including *The Mad Farmer Poems*, *Sex, Economy, Freedom and Community*, and *Our Only World*.

This isn't just a native issue. We're here protecting the water, not only for our families and our children, but for your families and your children. For every ranch and every farm along the Missouri River.

Mekasi Horinek

Mekasi Horinek is a member of the Ponca Nation who has fought against the ecological degradation wrought by the oil and natural gas industries. He spent six months organizing on the ground with the Water Protectors at Standing Rock.

Group protesting the lynching of four African Americans in Georgia, Washington, DC, 1947

Like slavery and apartheid,
poverty is not natural.
It is man-made and it can be
overcome and eradicated
by the actions of human beings.
And overcoming poverty
is not a gesture of charity.
It is an act of justice. It is
the protection of a fundamental
human right, the right
to dignity and a decent life.
While poverty persists,
there is no true freedom.

Nelson Mandela

Nelson Mandela (1918–2013) was a South African anti-apartheid leader
who led a campaign of peaceful, nonviolent protest against the government and
its policies. Mandela became the first Black president of South Africa from
1994 to 1999, after serving twenty-seven years in prison for political offenses.

HOUSING
IS A
HUMAN RIGHT.

THERE CAN BE NO FAIRNESS
OR JUSTICE IN A SOCIETY IN WHICH
SOME LIVE IN HOMELESSNESS,
OR IN THE SHADOW OF THAT RISK,
WHILE OTHERS
CANNOT EVEN IMAGINE IT.

Jordan Flaherty

Jordan Flaherty (1979–) is a writer, producer, and community organizer based in New Orleans. He was the first journalist to bring the case of the Jena Six to a national audience and has won awards for his post-Katrina reporting. He is author of *No More Heroes: Grassroots Responses to the Savior Mentality* and *Floodlines: Community and Resistance From Katrina to the Jena Six*.

We have reached a point
in history when we have the
technical capacities to
solve poverty, malnutrition,
inequality, and of course
global warming.

The deciding factors for
whether we take advantage
of our potential will be
our activism and
our international unity.

Eyal Weintraub

Eyal Weintraub (2000–) is an Argentinian
climate activist and cofounder
of Jóvenes por el Clima Argentina
(Youth for Climate Argentina).

Greta Thunberg, meeting of the European Parliment's climate committee, Brussels, Belgium, 2020

YES,

we are failing,
but there is still time
to turn everything around.
We can still fix this....
I want you to act
as if the house was on fire.
Because

IT IS.

Greta Thunberg

Greta Thunberg (2003–) is a Swedish environmental activist who has inspired
an international movement to fight climate change, beginning with her School Strike
for Climate outside the Swedish parliament at age fifteen. In 2019, to avoid flying,
she sailed across the Atlantic Ocean to the US to address the UN Climate Action Summit.

We don't have time to sit on our hands as our planet burns. For young people, climate change is bigger than election or reelection. It's life or death.

Alexandria Ocasio-Cortez

Alexandria Ocasio-Cortez (1989–), also known by her initials as AOC, is an American politician, electoral organizer, and activist serving as the US Representative for New York's 14th congressional district in the Bronx and Queens since 2019. She advocates for the working class over corporate interests, and works for social, racial, economic, and environmental justice.

WE DON'T HAVE A HIDDEN AGENDA.
THERE IS NO MONEY MOTIVATION.
WE WANT TO BREATHE CLEAN AIR,
WE WANT TO NOT GET KILLED IN OUR SCHOOLS,
WE WANT TO HAVE A PLANET THAT IS LIVABLE.

Jamie Margolin

Jamie Margolin (2001–) is a Colombian American youth
climate activist and a cofounder of Zero Hour, a climate
action organization based in Seattle, which organized
the 2018 Youth Climate March in Washington, DC.

Ban the Bomb group, protest against resumption of A-bomb tests by the United States, New York, NY, 1962

We are either going to have a future where women lead the way to make peace with the Earth or we are not going to have a human future at all.

Vandana Shiva

Vandana Shiva (1952–) is an Indian scholar, environmental activist, and food sovereignty and anti-globalization advocate. She is a leader and board member of the International Forum on Globalization and has authored more than twenty books, including *The Violence of the Green Revolution*.

Every successful social movement in this country's history has used disruption as a strategy to fight for social change.

Alicia Garza

Alicia Garza (1981–) is an Oakland-based organizer, civil rights activist, writer, and public speaker known for cofounding the Black Lives Matter movement. She currently directs special projects at the National Domestic Workers Alliance and is the principal at the Black Futures Lab.

I was a radical, a revolutionist.
I am still a revolutionist...
I am glad I was in the Stonewall riot.
I remember when someone
threw a Molotov cocktail, I thought,
"My god, the revolution is here.
The revolution is finally here!"

Sylvia Rivera

Sylvia Rivera (1951–2002) was a gay liberation and transgender rights activist in New York City in the 1960s and 1970s. Rivera, who identified as a drag queen, cofounded and participated in demonstrations with the Gay Liberation Front, including at the Stonewall Riots. She cofounded STAR (Street Transvestite Action Revolutionaries) with Marsha P. Johnson.

LOVE
CONQUERS
HATE
#orlando

JUNE 12th 2016

SAY THEIR NAMES

DAd
LO
M

Tribute to the victims of the Pulse Night Club Shooting,
Stonewall Inn, New York, NY, 2016

How can we tolerate a situation where the children or parents of the rich get the medical attention they need in order to stay alive, while members of

working-class families, who lack health insurance, have to die or needlessly suffer – or go hopelessly into debt to get the care they need?

Bernie Sanders

Bernie Sanders (1941–) has been an independent member of the United States Senate from Vermont since 2007 and was US Representative for the state's at-large congressional district from 1991 to 2007. He ran for the US Democratic Party nomination in the 2016 and 2020 presidential elections. He's an advocate of social democratic and progressive policies including single payer healthcare.

There are only two kinds of people in the world: the disabled, and the yet-to-be-disabled.

Ed Roberts

Ed Roberts (1939–1995) was an American disability rights activist. In 1962, Roberts became the first severely disabled student to attend the University of California at Berkeley. His lifelong work and advocacy championed the right of people with disabilities to lead independent lives.

DON'T BE IN A HURRY TO CONDEMN BECAUSE HE DOESN'T DO WHAT YOU DO OR THINK AS YOU THINK OR AS FAST.

THERE WAS A TIME WHEN YOU DIDN'T KNOW WHAT YOU KNOW TODAY.

Malcolm X

Malcolm X (1925–1965) was a minister, human rights activist, civil rights leader, and national spokesperson for the Nation of Islam in the 1950s and 1960s. Until his assassination in 1965, he supported Black nationalism and the fight against systematic racism by any means necessary, at times putting him at odds with nonviolent movements.

#InOurLifeTime we will fight for and alongside victims of gun violence, and we will prevail.

Emma González

Emma González (1999–) was a senior at Marjory Stoneman Douglas High School in Parkland, Florida, during the deadly school shooting of 2018. Since the attack, González has become a leader in the effort to spur social and legislative change around gun safety, cofounding the #NeverAgain gun-control movement and the advocacy group March For Our Lives.

I'M CONVINCED OF THIS: GOOD DONE ANYWHERE IS GOOD DONE EVERYWHERE.

Maya Angelou

Maya Angelou (1928–2014) was an American poet, autobiographer, storyteller, and civil rights activist, as well as a performing artist and director. She is author of *I Know Why the Caged Bird Sings* among many other books.

TO BE A REVOLUTIONARY YOU HAVE TO BE A HUMAN BEING,

YOU HAVE TO CARE ABOUT PEOPLE WHO HAVE NO POWER.

Jane Fonda

Jane Fonda (1937–) is an actress and winner of two Academy Awards.
She is a longtime civil rights and anti-war activist and cofounder of
the Women's Media Center. Inspired by Greta Thunberg, she has organized
the "Fire Drill Friday" climate change protests in Washington, DC.

It is the obligation of every person born in a safer room to open the door when someone in danger knocks.

Dina Nayeri

Dina Nayeri (1979–) is an Iranian American novelist, essayist, and short story writer. She is author of the novels *A Teaspoon of Earth and Sea* and *Refuge* and the nonfiction book *The Ungrateful Refugee*.

No pride for some of us without liberation for all of us.

Marsha P. Johnson

Marsha P. Johnson (1945–1992) was an American drag performer and gay liberation activist. Known as the Mayor of Christopher Street, Johnson was a notable figure of New York City's nightlife scene and a participant in the Stonewall uprising of 1969. As an AIDS activist, Johnson worked with ACT UP NYC.

Imprisonment... is a cruel and useless substitute for the elimination of those conditions—poverty, unemployment, homelessness, desperation, racism, greed—which are at the root of most punished crime. The crimes of the rich and powerful go mostly unpunished.

Howard Zinn

Howard Zinn (1922–2010) was a historian, playwright, and social activist. In addition to *A People's History of the United States*, he has written many books, including *You Can't Be Neutral on a Moving Train*, *The People Speak*, and *Passionate Declarations*.

Angela Y. Davis, 1974

[PRISON] RELIEVES US OF THE RESPONSIBILITY OF SERIOUSLY ENGAGING WITH THE PROBLEMS OF OUR SOCIETY, ESPECIALLY THOSE PRODUCED BY RACISM AND, INCREASINGLY, GLOBAL CAPITALISM.

Angela Y. Davis

Angela Y. Davis (1944–) is a scholar, writer, and radical Black educator and activist for civil rights and other social issues including the abolition of prisons. She has authored several books, including *Women, Race, and Class* and *Are Prisons Obsolete?*

THE LIBERATION OF THE EARTH, THE LIBERATION OF WOMEN, THE LIBERATION OF ALL HUMANITY IS THE NEXT STEP OF FREEDOM WE NEED TO WORK FOR, AND IT'S THE NEXT STEP OF PEACE THAT WE NEED TO CREATE.

Vandana Shiva

Vandana Shiva (1952–) is an Indian scholar, environmental activist, and food sovereignty and anti-globalization advocate. She is a leader and board member of the International Forum on Globalization has authored more than twenty books, including *The Violence of the Green Revolution*.

We are beginning to understand that the world is always being made fresh and never finished; that activism can be the journey rather than the arrival; that struggle doesn't always have to be confrontational but can take the form of reaching out to find common ground with the many others in our society who are also seeking ways out from alienation, isolation, privatization, and dehumanization by corporate globalization.

Grace Lee Boggs

Grace Lee Boggs (1915–2015) was a Chinese American author, social activist, philosopher, and intersectional feminist and a noted figure in Detroit's civil rights and Black Power movements. She is author of *The Next American Revolution: Sustainable Activism for the Twenty-First Century*.

YOU HAVE TO ACT AS IF IT WERE POSSIBLE TO RADICALLY TRANSFORM THE WORLD.

AND YOU HAVE TO DO IT ALL THE TIME.

Angela Y. Davis

Angela Y. Davis (1944–) is a scholar, writer, and radical Black educator and activist for civil rights and other social issues including the abolition of prisons. She has authored several books, including *Women, Race, and Class* and *Are Prisons Obsolete?*

Civil disobedience—

*the willingness to stand
in the way of injustice
and put oneself on the line*

—is an act of love.

Tim DeChristopher

Tim DeChristopher (1981–) disrupted an illegitimate Bureau of Land Management oil and gas auction in December of 2008 by posing as a bidder and outbidding oil companies for parcels of land. He was sentenced to two years in federal prison. He has since coorganized the climate justice organization Peaceful Uprising and most recently the Climate Disobedience Center.

Rachel Carson, 1962

The question is whether any civilization can wage relentless war on life without destroying itself, and without losing the right to be called civilized.

Rachel Carson

Rachel Carson (1907–1964) was a writer, ecologist, and conservationist whose book *Silent Spring* warned of the dangers of chemical pesticides, catalyzing the global environmental movement and leading to the creation of United States Environmental Protection Agency.

This is my charge
to everyone.
We have to be better.
We have to love more,
hate less.
We've gotta listen more
and talk less.
We gotta know that
this is everybody's
responsibility.

Megan Rapinoe

Megan Rapinoe (1985–) is a professional soccer player
for the team OL Reign and cocaptain of the US National
Team. She is an advocate for LGBTQ+ rights and equal pay,
and cofounder of a gender-neutral lifestyle brand.

For me, forgiveness and compassion are always linked: How do we hold people accountable for wrongdoing and yet at the same time remain in touch with their humanity enough to believe in their capacity to be transformed?

bell hooks

bell hooks (1952–) is an author, professor, feminist, and social activist whose work has examined intersectional feminism, Black masculinity, race and class, and community. She is author of *Ain't I A Woman: Black Women and Feminism*, *Bone Black: Memories of Girlhood*, and *The Will to Change: Men, Masculinity, and Love*.

There is no sound so sweet
as the sound of chains
that held folks back for so long
falling noisily to the ground.
And it's still true:
Once we can reimagine and
resist in significant numbers,

WE WILL RISE AGAIN,

reaching new heights and
setting better foundations
for living and loving,
for building a new world.

Bill Ayers

Bill Ayers (1944–) was a leader of the Weather Underground, which
opposed US involvement in the Vietnam War in the 1960s. He lived
underground for ten years, an experience he described in *Fugitive Days*,
and is now a school reform activist and professor of education.

Once, people believed in human sacrifice.
    Not anymore.
Once, people believed in slavery.
    Not anymore.
Once, people believed that women were
not as capable as men.
    Not anymore.
I hope one day we'll be able to say,
"Once, people believed in war.
    Not anymore."

Frances Crowe

Frances Crowe (1919–2019) was
a Quaker and lifelong peace activist
and pacifist from the Pioneer
Valley of Western Massachusetts.

TO HOPE

IS TO GIVE YOURSELF TO THE FUTURE, AND THAT COMMITMENT TO THE FUTURE MAKES THE PRESENT INHABITABLE.

Rebecca Solnit

Rebecca Solnit (1961–) is a writer, historian, and activist who has written twenty books on feminism, Western and Indigenous history, popular power, social change and insurrection, and more. She is author of *Hope in the Dark*, *A Paradise Built in Hell*, and *Men Explain Things to Me*.

Not everything that is faced can be changed, but nothing can be changed until it is faced.

James Baldwin

James Baldwin (1924–1987) was a novelist, essayist, playwright, and activist of the American civil rights movement. He is the author of many books, including *Notes of a Native Son*, *The Fire Next Time*, and *Go Tell It on the Mountain*.

Black Lives Matter Plaza, Washington, DC, 2020

Published by
Princeton Architectural Press
202 Warren Street
Hudson, New York 12534
www.papress.com

ISBN 978-1-61689-996-7

Production editor: Parker Menzimer
Design: Benjamin English

Library of Congress Control Number: 2020942295

Page 82. *So You Want to Talk About Race* by Ijeoma Oluo,
copyright © 2018, 2019. Reprinted by permission of Seal Press,
an imprint of Hachette Book Group, Inc.

Image Credits
14. Library of Congress, LC-DIG-ppmsca-08102
20. Library of Congress, LC-DIG-ds-07432
24. VOA / Public domain
30. Library of Congress, LC-DIG-ppmsca-40912
36. Library of Congress, LC-DIG-ds-07266
42–43. Mondalawy / Wikimedia Commons / CC BY-SA 4.0
46. Library of Congress, LC-DIG-ppmsca-65038
52. Library of Congress, LC-DIG-hec-04900
56. Library of Congress, LC-USZ62-122985
64–65. Pax Ahimsa Gethen / CC BY-SA 4.0
70. Matthew T Rader / CC BY-SA 4.0
78. Library of Congress, LC-DIG-ds-02975
84. Library of Congress, LC-DIG-ppmsca-38857
86. Library of Congress, LC-USZ62-101762
102. Library of Congress, LC-DIG-ds-07416
106. European Parliament / CC BY 2.0
110. Library of Congress, LC-USZ62-126854
114–15. Rhododendrites / Wikimedia Commons / CC BY-SA 4.0
126. Philippe Halsman / Public domain
132. Smithsonian Institution from United States / No restrictions
140. Annettet / Wikimedia Commons / CC BY-SA 4.0

Front and Back Cover
March for Our Lives rally protesting gun violence, Washington, DC,
March 24, 2018. Photographs by Phil Roeder